A CLASSICAL CHRISTMAS

ISBN 1-57560-261-X

Visit our website at www.cherrylane.com

CONTENTS

4 ANGELS WE HAVE HEARD ON HIGH

5 AVE MARIA (BACH/GOUNOD)

8 AVE MARIA (SCHUBERT)

14 BRING A TORCH, JEANETTE, ISABELLA

11 CHINESE DANCE from *THE NUTCRACKER*

18 DANCE OF THE REED FLUTES from *THE NUTCRACKER*

16 DANCE OF THE SUGAR PLUM FAIRY from *THE NUTCRACKER*

21 EVENING PRAYER from *HÄNSEL AND GRETEL*

22 THE FIRST NOËL

24 GESU BAMBINO

27 GOD REST YE MERRY, GENTLEMEN

28 HALLELUJAH! from *MESSIAH*

33 HARK! THE HERALD ANGELS SING

34 HE SHALL FEED HIS FLOCK from *MESSIAH*

36 IT CAME UPON A MIDNIGHT CLEAR

38 JESU, JOY OF MAN'S DESIRING

46 JOY TO THE WORLD

48 MARCH from *THE NUTCRACKER*

41 MARCH OF THE TOYS from *BABES IN TOYLAND*

52 O CHRISTMAS TREE

53 O COME, ALL YE FAITHFUL

54 O HOLY NIGHT

60 O JESUS, SO SWEET

58 PASTORAL SYMPHONY from *MESSIAH*

61 RUSSIAN DANCE from *THE NUTCRACKER*

64 SHEEP MAY SAFELY GRAZE

80 SILENT NIGHT

72 SINFONIA from *CHRISTMAS ORATORIO*

74 SUSSEX CAROL

76 WALTZ OF THE FLOWERS from *THE NUTCRACKER*

Angels We Have Heard On High

Traditional French Carol

Ave Maria

By Charles Gounod
based on "Prelude in C" by Johann Sebastian Bach

Moderately slow

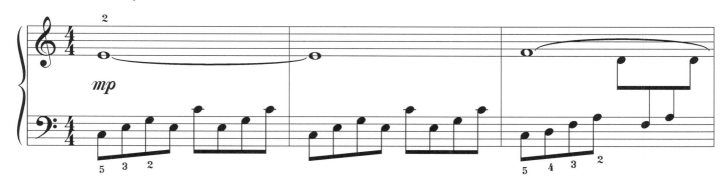

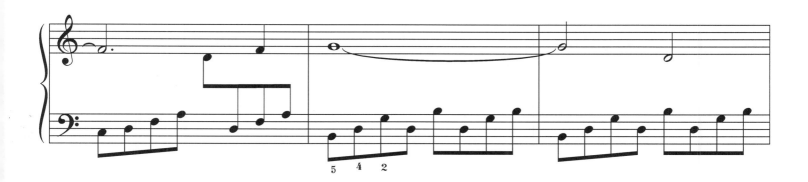

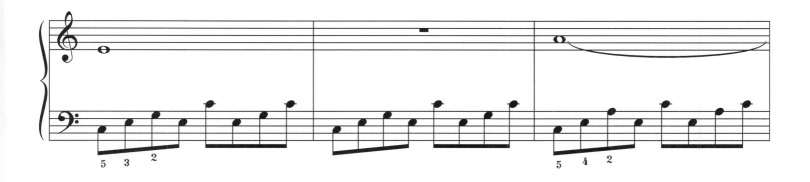

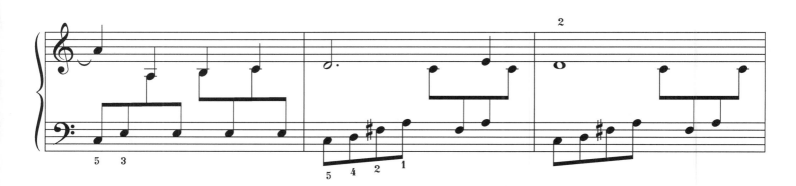

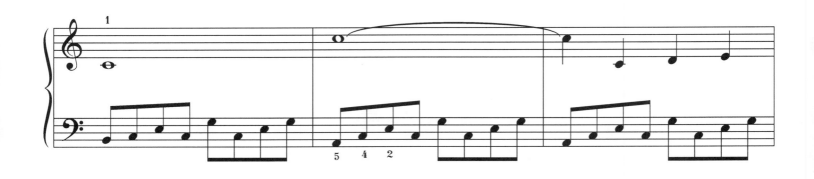

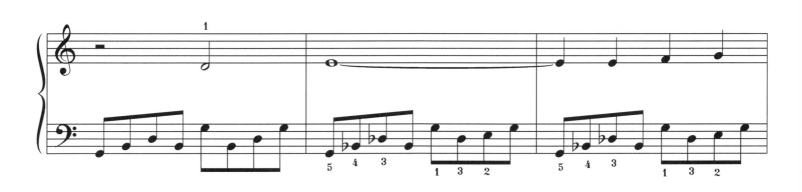

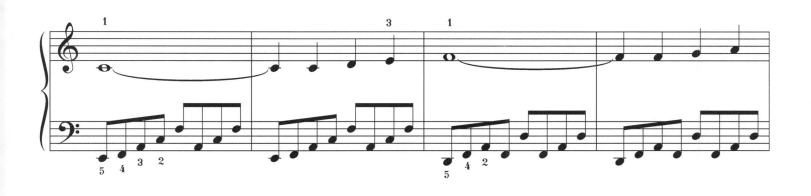

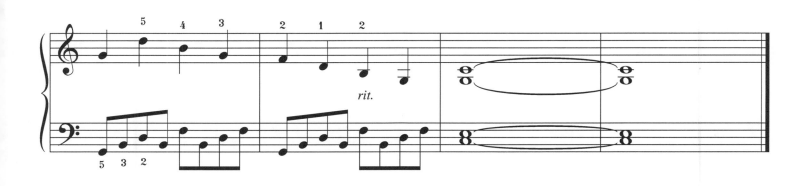

Ave Maria

By Franz Schubert

Slowly

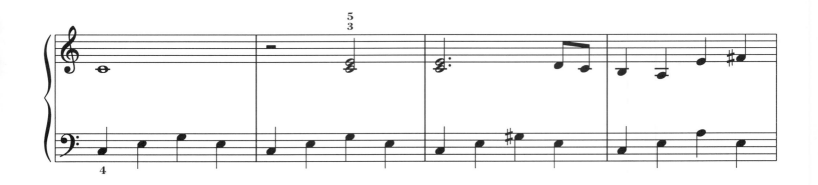

Chinese Dance
from THE NUTCRACKER

By Pyotr Il'yich Tchaikovsky

Bring A Torch, Jeannette, Isabella

17th Century French Provençal Carol

Moderately, flowing

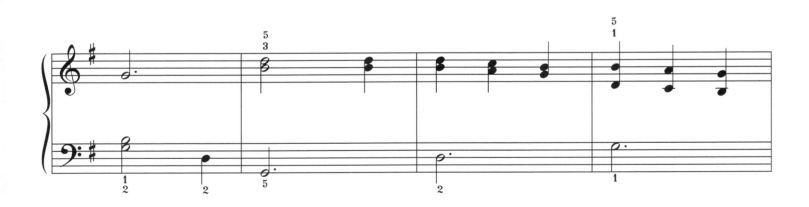

Dance of the Sugar Plum Fairy

from THE NUTCRACKER

By Pyotr Il'yich Tchaikovsky

Dance of the Reed Flutes
from THE NUTCRACKER

By Pyotr Il'yich Tchaikovsky

Moderately slow

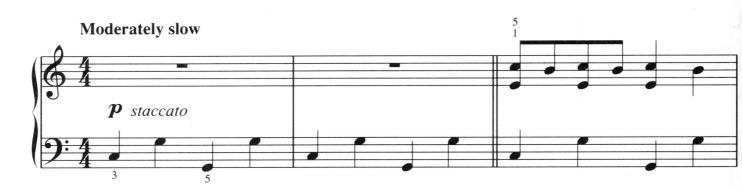

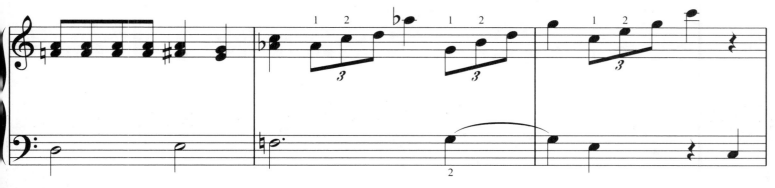

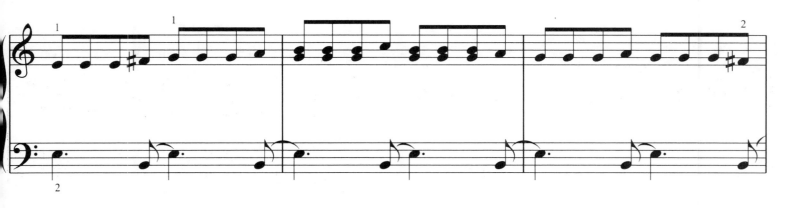

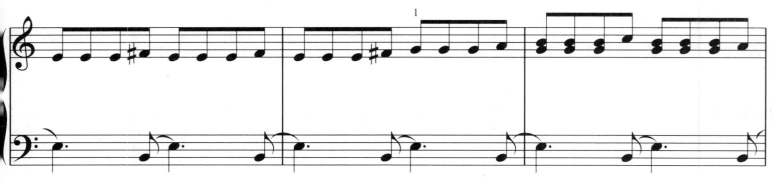

Evening Prayer

from HANSEL AND GRETEL

By Engelbert Humperdinck

21

The First Noël

17th Century English Carol
Music from W. Sandys' *Christmas Carols*

Moderately

Gesu Bambino

Music by Pietro Yon

Slowly, but in 2 (♩. = 1 beat)

Not too slow

God Rest Ye Merry, Gentlemen

19th Century English Carol

Moderately fast

Hallelujah!

from MESSIAH

By George Frideric Handel

Majestically

Hark! The Herald Angels Sing

Music by Felix Mendelssohn-Bartholdy
Arranged by William H. Cummings

With spirit

He Shall Feed His Flock

from MESSIAH

Music by George Frideric Handel

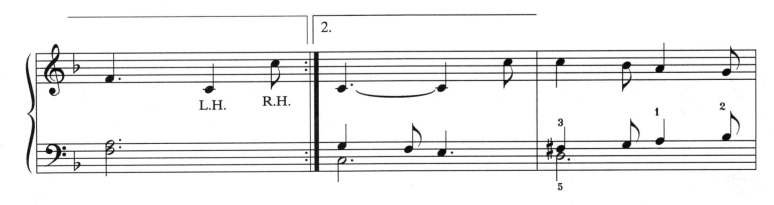

It Came Upon A Midnight Clear

Traditional English Melody
Adapted by Arthur Sullivan

Jesu, Joy of Man's Desiring

By Johann Sebastian Bach

March of the Toys

By Victor Herbert

Strict March Tempo

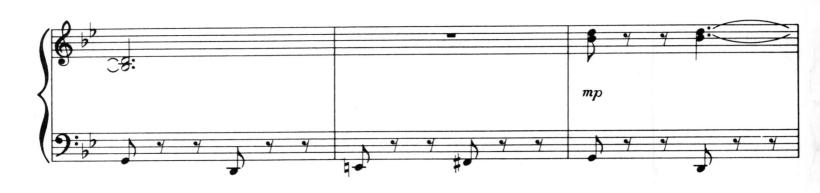

43

Joy to the World

Music by George Frederick Handel
Arranged by Lowell Mason

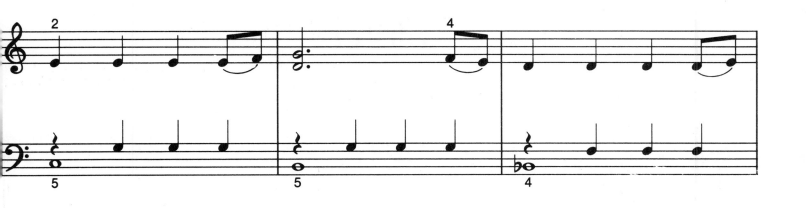

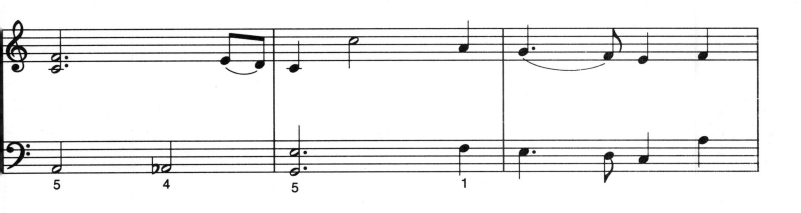

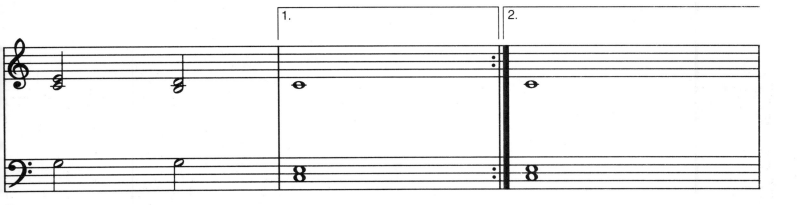

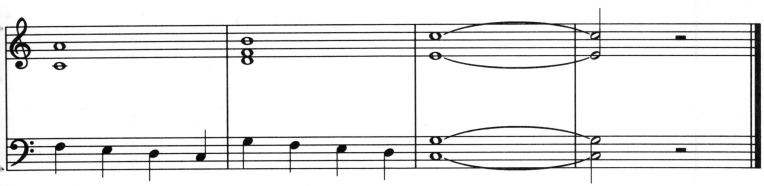

March
from THE NUTCRACKER

By Pyotr Il'yich Tchaikovs[

Moderately (in two)

D.C. al Coda

CODA

O Christmas Tree

Traditional German Carol

Moderately

O Come, All Ye Faithful

Music by John Francis Wade

O Holy Night

Music by Adolfe Adam

Moderately, flowing

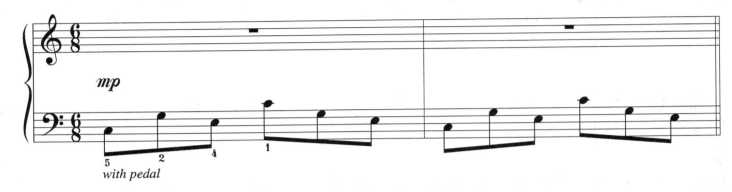

Pastoral Symphony
from MESSIAH

By George Frideric Handel

Moderately slow

O Jesus So Sweet

17th Century German Hymn

Moderately slow

Russian Dance
from THE NUTCRACKER

By Pyotr Il'yich Tchaikovsky

Moderately fast

Sheep May Safely Graze

Johann Sebastian Bach
1685-1750

Andante

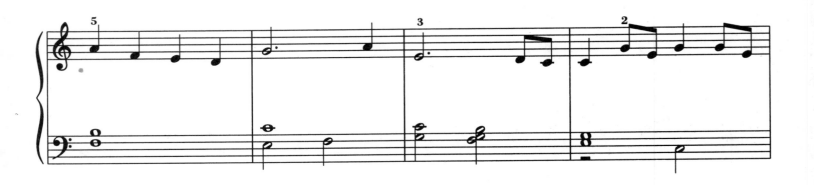

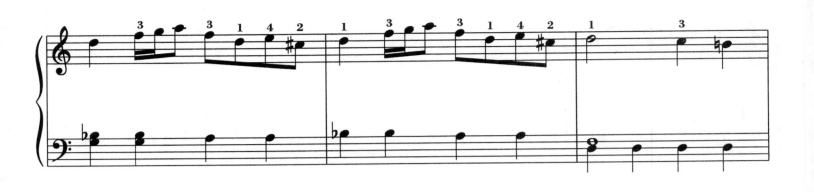

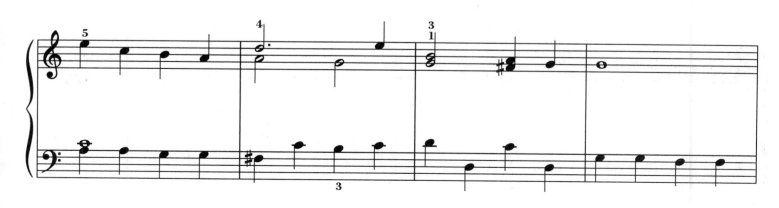

Sinfonia
from CHRISTMAS ORATORIO

By Johann Sebastian Bach

Moderately slow

Sussex Carol

Traditional English Carol

Moderately slow

Waltz of the Flowers
from THE NUTCRACKER

By Pyotr Il'yich Tchaikovsky

Moderately

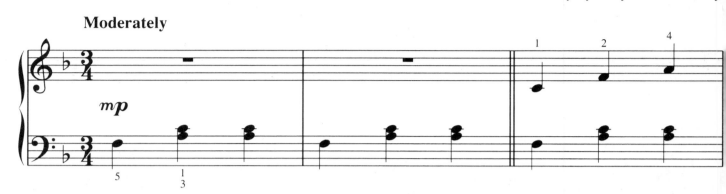

Silent Night

Music by Franz X. Gruber